alive Natural Health Guides 36

Elysa Markowitz

Smoothies
and
other scrumptious
delights

alive
BOOKS
Vancouver
Canada

Contents

All About Smoothies

Note: Conversions in this book (from imperial to metric) are not exact. They have been rounded to the nearest measurement for convenience. Exact measurements are given in imperial. The recipes in this book are by no means to be taken as therapeutic. They simply promote the philosophy of both the author and *alive* Books in relation to whole foods, health and nutrition, while incorporating the practical advice given by the author in the first section of the book.

Smoothies Recipes

54   40   30

> **"The only ones among you who will be really happpy are those who have sought and found how to serve"**
>
> Albert Einstein

All about Smoothies and blending

Introduction . . . .

Start your family's day the smoothie way!

Welcome to the world of blending. Picture a typical morning — you have 10 minutes to prepare and eat breakfast and get out the door, and feed your family a healthy meal. Is it possible? Yes, and the answer is here — blend. When you blend your own smoothies (as well as sauces, soups, salsas, dressings, and desserts) you can choose the best quality ingredients and prepare them in a few minutes. Whole organic foods build healthier bodies because they contain more nutrients and more enzymes. Blending makes it convenient to choose the best for your health. Be creative — the recipes in this book give you a place to start. You may alter them to suit your health needs, and your tastes. If an ingredient is not available in your area, substitute one that is, or ask your local health food store to order it for you. You can also use the resource page at the back of this book to find companies that will send their products right to your door.

> **"The human body is the universe in miniature. That which cannot be found in the body is not to be found in the universe, Hence the philosopher's formula, that the universe within reflects the universe without. It follows, therefore, that if our knowledge of our own body could be perfect, we would know the universe."**
>
> Mahatma Ghandhi

About Blenders . . . .

This book will help you get the most from your blender. From small to large, there are many styles of blenders on the market. Some blenders come with plastic blending jars, some with glass. I prefer plastic — it's lighter, and more durable. Some motors are very powerful; others will burn out if used beyond their capacity. With any blender, always start with the liquid ingredients and blend those first, then add the solid and more concentrated ingredients.

The Tribest Personal Blender

The recipes and methods in this book were developed for the two-cup blender jar of the Tribest Personal Blender. If for any reason you want to make more, or less, simply adapt the recipe. Half, double or triple the recipes to fit your needs.

I prefer the Tribest Personal Blender because it is compact and takes up less counter space. This blender has individual blending cups so you can make your smoothie, cover the container, wash the blade, walk out the door with your meal, and let the next family member make their own breakfast — also in the blender. Don't be deceived by size, the motor is power- *The Tribest* ful enough (200 watts, ¼ horsepower) to make a wide variety *Personal Blender* of recipes. It can crush ice, blend fresh, soaked, dried, and frozen ingredients, make almond flour, and turn flax into a fine meal in moments.

The entire blender, even when filled with ingredients, is so light (less than three pounds) that I can shake the entire unit when I want to move the ingredients from the top towards the blade on the bottom. Picture me jumping up and down in a shake and blend routine, singing Latin songs, as I make my blender meals.

Don't limit the Tribest Personal Blender to your kitchen — take it with you to the office, or on trips. With an adaptor you can plug it into your car lighter and make smoothies on the road — literally. This is very useful when there are no healthy restaurants in sight. Pack the desired ingredients in a cooler, blend, and you have a healthy meal in moments — right there in your car. Just don't forget to pull over first!

Easy Cleaning

Cleaning any blender is made easier by putting some soapy water into the blender, pulsing (turning it on for short bursts), and rinsing. Most blenders have a pulse button. The Tribest Personal Blender can be pulsed by pushing the blender container down, not turning it clockwise into the continuous "on" position.

Versatility of the Blender

A blender is a very versatile tool. It has many functions. Below is a partial list of what this appliance can do:

Tribest Personal Blender, the quickest and easiest to operate.

- **Blend** whole foods (not to be confused with "juicing" whole foods — the definition of juicing is to separate pulp from liquid — a blender will never do this kind of separation)
- **Chop** fruits, vegetables, and cheese to fine in seconds
  - **Crack** nuts, seeds, and grains (not all blenders can do this)
  - **Crumb** breads and crackers for crusts, coatings
  - **Crush** ice in seconds
  - **Dice** into salsas — with quick pulsing action
  - **Emulsify** ingredients for dressings, sauces
    - **Frappe** drinks — designer coffees, and non-caffeinated choices
  - **Grind** grains, herbs and spices
- **Homogenize** frozen drinks and deserts
- **Mill** grains, beans into flour
- **Mince** herbs and vegetables for pesto and more
- **Prepare** non-dairy milks (from nuts and seeds or fruits)
- **Puree** puddings, baby foods
- **Wet chop** fruits and vegetables into slaws

Operating the Tribest Personal Blender . . . .

To make recipes in this blender simply fill, cover, and push down. This appliance is extremely user-friendly because there are no buttons or dials, or awkward parts to clean. The Tribest Personal Blender comes with three containers:

- one cup (225 ml) grinding container, perfect for baby foods, small amounts, or herb and spice mixtures
- two cup (450 ml) blending container, recommended for most liquid recipes
- XL three cup (675 ml) container for lighter, more liquid ingredients.

There are two choices of blades, one for grinding solids, and one for blending liquids. The blade for dry ingredients has two prongs. This can be used for grinding nuts, seeds, spices, or herbs. The blade for wet ingredients has four prongs. This is intended to be used for crushing ice and making recipes that combine both wet and dry ingredients, like smoothies.

Either blade can be used with any size cup. For some recipes it is suggested that you shake the entire unit to keep the ingredients moving and blending evenly.

Operation Guidelines:

1 Plug machine motor into desired outlet (wall or inverter) and remove lid (if covered).

2 Fill blender container with desired ingredients and choose desired blade bottom (two pronged for dry ingredients, four pronged for wet ingredients):

A One cup container (grinding container): use a maximum of ½ cup (125 ml) liquid, ¼ cup (50 ml) solids, or ¾ cup (175 ml) dry ingredients — herbs, spices, grains, nuts, etc.

B Two cup container (blender container): use at least ¼ cup (50 ml) liquid for any recipe — up to one and ¼ cup (300 ml) maximum liquid; for dry ingredients up to one and ¼ cup (300 ml). Shake occasionally to keep ingredients moving.

C Three cup container (XL Cup): use a maximum of two cups (500 ml) liquid and ½ cup (125 ml) solids for the three cup container; not recommended for dry ingredients unless very light (may be used to mince greens and make flax or sesame meal).

Personal Blender showing grinder base.

3 Cover the blender container with the desired blade assembly and turn in a clockwise motion to seal completely, invert and place into the motor base.

4 Turn the blender container to fit into small notch (groove), once in place press down. For pulsing press down and release. For continuous use, press down and turn blender container to the right (clockwise) until you hear a click.

5 The machine will stay on until you press down and turn to the left (counter clockwise). This stops the blending.

6 Lift blender container off and turn it onto its top side, to open the blade assembly. Remove blade assembly by turning counter clockwise. Pour into the serving container, or use the container and lid as a serving and storing container.

7 Rinse parts, and store for next use.

The beauty of this blender is that there are no buttons to push, no rubber rings to remove to clean the blade bottoms, and no glass jars to shatter. You have your own container, your own lid, and your own choice of ingredients. The next member of your family can make their recipe the way they want, using the blade they want, in their own container and lid. Blending this way is simple, convenient, and fast.

Blender Safety

As with any kitchen appliance, unplug your blender when not in use for safety reasons. I once had a blender turn itself on (it shorted electrically). Luckily I was home, heard a grinding noise in the kitchen, and hurried in to see smoke coming out of the blender motor. Immediately I unplugged it. It was about to catch on fire. Now, I plug my kitchen appliances into a power strip and turn off the power to the strip when not in use.

Preparing to Blend . . . .

Basic whole foods

Blended whole foods make simple and tasty meals for everyone. Picking fresh tomatoes and blending them into a soup consistency can be a heavenly dish — no spice is required when foods are flavorful. Spices, salt and sugar are often needed when foods are missing their natural flavors, or when the palate has become jaded.

Fresh fruits rarely need sweeteners. On occasion I have had a sour strawberry and enjoyed maple cream or dates as a sweetener. However, from rich, organic soil I have tasted strawberries so sweet, to add anything would have been unnecessary.

Local markets are a great resource of seasonal variety.

Organic, Seasonal, Local

Choosing the right ingredients is the first step in getting the most from your blender. First, and foremost, find organic food sources. Whether you grow your own, find a farmer's market in your area, support local health food stores that stock organic produce and foods, or order from a organic delivery service — find a way to get organic food. When I lived in New Mexico, I would drive 160 miles to buy organic foods. It was well worth the trip. Whole, natural, organic foods are more nutritious, with more vitamins and minerals, and have no pesticide residue.

Second, eat in season and choose foods grown locally whenever possible. Most of the recipes in this book don't require cooking, so you receive the full benefit of the live enzymes found in fresh fruits and vegetables. When the fall rolls around, I look forward to fresh corn and persimmons. Yams are moist, and apples have just been picked (otherwise, they can be in storage for a year or more). Tomatoes have more flavor when picked in the autumn after a full summer's sunshine. Winter brings root vegetables as well as so many varieties of squash. Summer blesses us with fruits in such variety and abundance: soft fruits, berries, melons — heaven here on earth.

Take advantage of fresh local produce.

You have probably noticed that in season, locally grown produce is fresher, with a more vibrant flavor than produce available year round. Just compare the fragrance of a freshly picked garden tomato to that of its pale, supermarket relative. When food is sold out of season, it is often shipped from another country, and unfortunately, picked too early in order to prevent bruising and spoilage. Too often this produce is grown with pesticides no longer allowed in North America, but still sold to other countries.

Choosing organic produce helps the farmers, the workers who pick the food, the shippers who handle the food, and ultimately, us, when we eat the food. It is time to stop waging chemical warfare on the planet. When we choose organic, the air gets cleaner, the insects come into balance, and we can avoid the ground water being contaminated with excess nitrates and other unnecessary toxic chemicals — sprayed or otherwise used.

Create your Own Recipes . . . .

By combining ingredients from the following categories you can learn to create your own recipes. Start with the one or more ingredients from the first category, blend and taste. Then add a liquid from the next category, blend and taste, and finally, if you desire, add flavor enhancers and nutritional supplements from the last category — then blend and taste. When you make recipes this way, you can taste what you like, or don't. This book is intended to encourage your creativity. Enjoy making your own unique smoothies, sauces and soups.

Fruit Smoothies

Category 1: Fresh or frozen fruits — use ½ cup (125 ml) of any of the following:

Winter: apples, pears, persimmons, grapes, pomegranates

Citrus: grapefruit, blood oranges, oranges, tangelos, tangerines, lemons, limes

Summer fruits: apples, grapes, soft-pitted fruit (apricots, nectarines, peaches, plums), berries (blueberries, huckleberries, mulberries, raspberries, strawberries)

Tropical: kiwi, mangoes, papayas, pineapples

Exotic: cheramoya, colostrum columbarum, mame, sapote (some of these fruits are found in tropical climates, like Florida, or Thailand)

Locally grown seasonal fruit

Category 2: Liquid or juice — use ½ to 1 cup (125 to 250 ml) (adjust to create desired thickness) of any o0f the following:

Juices: apple, beet (in small amounts) cherry, coconut, cranberry, mango nectar orange, papaya nectar, pineapple, pomegranate, or other fresh fruit juice *

* *Please read labels — too many bottled juices have unnecessary added sugar. Find fresh, unpasteurized juice whenever possible, squeeze your own if you can. It should be noted that unpasteurized products have not been heated to kill potentially harmful bacteria. Caution should be taken that juice is fresh and from a reputable source, especially when given to children, the elderly, and those with compromised immune systems.*

Other liquids: dairy milks (cow or goat — organic whenever possible, raw is best when available, please see previous note about unpasteurized products), non-dairy milks (almond, oat, rice, soy, sunflower, etc.), plain yogurt, filtered water (hot or cold), ice cubes

Category 3: Thickeners — 2 tablespoons to ¼ cup (25 – 50 ml) of any of the following:

Bananas (fresh or frozen, ½ to whole depending on desired thickness)

Soaked dried fruits (without sulfur dioxide whenever possible) — try apples, apricots (Turkish are the best), unsweetened cherries, dates, figs, papaya, pears, and pineapple. You can also use some of the soaking water as a liquid and sweetener.

Nuts (raw if possible): almonds, Brazil, macadamia, pecans, pine nuts, pistachio, walnuts

Nut butters (raw if possible): almond, cashew, hazelnut, hemp, macadamia

Seeds (soak and rinse seeds when appropriate): chia, flax, hemp, pumpkin, sesame, sunflower

Oils: almond, coconut, flaxseed, grapeseed, hemp seed, olive, sesame, sunflower

Miso: mellow yellow or mellow white work best with fruit combinations

Category 4: Flavor enhancers, supplements and sweeteners — These ingredients are optional, used to add nutritional value and flavor. Add to taste, or use 1-3 tablespoons (15 – 50 ml) of the following:

Flavor Enhancers: black cherry concentrate, tart cherry concentrate, coconut, cocoa powder, edible essential oils such as cinnamon, ginger, fennel, mint, (1 - 3 drops maximum), flower essences (such as orange blossom, rose petal and lavender), mixed dried fruits, raw carob powder

Supplements: aloe juice, chia gel, Phi-plus (76 blended whole food ingredients) Barley max, spirulina, chlorella, blended green powders, protein powders, liquid minerals, Emergen-C (one packet), lecithin, bee pollen, MSM, royal jelly, sprouts (clover, alfalfa, sunflower, buckwheat), rice bran solubles, colostrum, bee pollen

Sweeteners: These are the least needed ingredients since fruit is usually sweet enough alone. The following are included for those with a sweet tooth. Add to taste: Agave nectar, black strap molasses, date sugar, raw honey, malt barley, grade B maple syrup, maple cream, maple sugar, rapadura (squeeze dried cane juice), rice syrup, stevia (liquid or powder), sorghum, sucanat, or other natural sweetener

Vegetable Smoothies, Savory Dressings, Soups, and Sauces

Category 1: Vegetables — ½ cup (125 ml) of any of the following:

Beets, broccoli, cabbage, carrots, cauliflower, celery, corn, cucumbers, daikon (Japanese radish), radish, sweet potatoes, tomatoes, yams

Leafy greens: arugula, beet greens, butter leaf lettuce, romaine lettuce, spinach, or other wild or cultivated greens

Summer squash: green zucchini, yellow squash

Other local, seasonal vegetables

Category 2: Liquid or juice — use ½ to 1 cup (125 – 250 ml) (adjust to create desired thickness) of any of the following:

Vegetable juices: carrot, green juices of choice (greens, celery, cabbage, spinach, cucumber, etc.), juice of rosemary, oregano, or sage

Liquids: dairy milks (cow or goat - organic whenever possible, raw is best where found), non-dairy milks (almond, rice, soy, sunflower, oat, etc.), plain yoghurt, filtered water (hot or cold)

Category 3: Thickeners — 2 tablespoons to ¼ cup (25 - 50 ml) of any of the following:

Avocado, dried tomatoes, nutritional yeast (Red Star), olives, psyllium

Nut butters (raw if possible): almond, cashew, hazelnut, hemp, macadamia

Nuts (raw if possible): almonds, Brazil, macadamia, pecans, pine nuts, pistachio, walnuts

Seeds (soak and rinse seeds when appropriate): chia, flax, hemp, pumpkin, sesame, sunflower

Oils: almond, coconut, flaxseed, grapeseed, hemp seed, olive, sesame, sunflower

Miso: red, barley, brown rice, dandelion leek, azuki, millet, or other savory miso flavors

Category 4: Flavor enhancers and supplements — These ingredients are optional, used to add nutritional value or flavor. Add to taste or use 1-3 tablespoons (15 – 50 ml) of the following ingredients:

Flavor Enhancers: coconut meat, edible essential oils (1 - 3 drops maximum) such as ginger, oregano, rosemary, sage, and lavender, raw carob powder, Veggielicious (plain and spiced — 11 dried veggies)

Supplements: Aloe juice, Barley max, Spirulina, Chlorella, Blended Green Powders, Protein powders, Liquid minerals, unsweetened varieties of Emergen-C (one packet), Rice bran solubles, lecithin, Royal Jelly, Sprouts (clover, alfalfa, sunflowe, buckwheat), rice bran solubles, colostrum, sea vegetables: powdered dulse, kelp, or nori

It was exciting to discover the many benefits of these super-foods while researching this book. Please use this as a reference section. If you have any difficulty finding any of the following foods, consult the resource section in the back of this book, or ask your local health food store to order them for you.

Aloe Juice

Aloe juice is best used raw. Aloe balances and enhances the body's systems at the cellular level, promoting tissue growth and regeneration. It is very helpful in strengthening and healing digestion. Aloe is especially useful to metabolism and the respiratory, immune, and circulatory systems. Aloe juice contains nine of the 10 essential amino acids, as well as essential fatty acids and plant sterols, which have natural anti-inflammatory properties.

Choose the best ingredients for super taste.

Bee Pollen

This bee product is rich in vitamin B12, has a full range of nutrients required by humans, improves endurance, helps in recovery from chronic illnesses, and is a remedy for allergies and hay fever.

Carob Powder (raw)

Carob is an alkaline fruit, rich in calcium and other minerals. Carob calms nervousness, helps in caffeine withdrawal, and conditions the bowels. Carob is a warming food, helpful in reversing cold in the body.

Coconut (raw)

Both the milk and meat contain a healthy saturated fat. Coconut milk works best for blending, as it requires fewer enzymes to be digested, and is high in caprylic acid, which is an anti-fungal (yeast fighting properties), anti-microbial, and anti-viral compound. Coconut helps the liver to lower cholesterol levels, stimulates thyroid function, aids in poor digestion (especially liver or gall bladder problems), lowers body need for omega 3 fatty acids and normalizes blood sugar.

Blended spices

Fresh herbs can be ground into tasty additions to soups or dressings. In my garden I grow sweet basil, parsley, and mint, which are tasty when minced. I have enjoyed making the following spice mixtures in the 1 cup (250 ml) blender, with the dry blade (two pronged). Use them in soups, salads, dips, and wherever you like.

Gomasio

2 parts hulled sesame seeds
1 part granulated garlic
½ part kelp
½ part sea salt

Lemon Peppered Flax Meal

1 part ground flaxseed (flax meal)
½ part lemon pepper (Mrs. Dash makes a great one)
¼ part sea salt

Papaya Seed Pepper

Papaya Seeds
Using a dehydrator, dry seeds at 105 degrees
Blend and store in spice jar with shaker top.

Peppered Parsley

1 part dehydrated parsley
½ part granulated garlic
¼ part dehydrated or freeze-dried onions

Spiced Sugar

2 parts rapadura or sucanat (or other sugar)
1 part powdered cinnamon
¼ part ground nutmeg
⅛ part ground cardamom

"Milk" can be made from non-animal sources. Almonds, pumpkin, sesame, and sunflower seeds make a tasty milk. Nut and seeds require soaking ahead of time, so keep some pre-soaked in the freezer for convenience.

> **one part soaked, rinsed, nut or seed**
> **2 parts water**
> Blend well. For a creamer consistency, add:
> **I banana, or**
> **I - 2 teaspoons** (15 –25 ml) **coconut oil**

This blended drink can be strained or kept as is. Nut or seed milk is great in smoothies, or poured over hot or cold whole grains, porridge or cereals. When the pulp is removed, the drink is more like dairy milk. Pour through a cheesecloth or a very fine strainer to remove the pulp.

You can flavor the milk with fresh vanilla bean, cinnamon, nutmeg, fresh or powdered ginger root, or essential oils of cinnamon or ginger to make interesting variations on the basic recipe. Almond, coconut, or maple extract, as well as tart cherry concentrate are also tasty choices. Sweeten to taste, with agave nectar, black strap molasses, maple syrup, raw honey, or stevia. Blend the flavoring and/or the sweetener after straining out the pulp.

Can be served warmed or chilled.

Nut and seed milks keep in the refrigerator for two to three days.

A nutritious dip or "cheeze" can be made from seeds or nuts. It is as simple as blending the soaked, rinsed seeds or nuts in water and letting them ferment on the counter overnight.

> Blend:
> **2 cups** (500 ml) **soaked sunflower, pumpkin,**
>   **sesame, or raw cashews,**
> Or any combination these choices
> **2 cups** (500 ml) **water** (use a bit more water
>   for a wetter cheeze)

16

For wetter cheeze:

Pour mixture into glass jar, cover with a towel, and let sit on counter overnight or 8 hours at a moderate room temperature (less than 95 degrees). Cheeze is ready after eight to 12 hours of sitting out. Spoon the solid off the top; discard the liquid on the bottom. Store in the refrigerator. It will approximately four to five days.

For thicker, drier cheeze:

Use less water, just enough to move in the blender, not enough to form a sauce. The blended seeds or nuts should be the consistency of pudding. Pour mixture into a colander lined with cheesecloth and put a heavy weight on top to press out any moisture. I use a glass gallon jug filled with water as a weight. Cover with cloth and let ferment overnight.

For either version:

For a savory cheeze, spice to taste with 2 - 4 tbsp (25 − 50 ml) Red Star nutritional yeast, and 1 - 2 tbsp (15 − 25 ml) red or barley miso. You can also add a drop of savory essential oils like fennel, rosemary, or sage. Serve as a paté, spread on celery, in pepper boats, or with flax crackers and bread.

For a sweet cheeze add 2 - 4 tbsp (25 − 50 ml) maple syrup, or agave nectar and 1 - 2 tsp (15 − 25 ml) mellow or light miso, a dash or cinnamon or nutmeg, or a splash of tart cherry concentrate. You can also add a drop of edible essential like cinnamon or ginger. Serve as a dip with dried fruit "chips," or stuff into dates for a sweet treat.

Unrefined Essential Oils provide nutritional and healing properties.

Edible Essential Oils

Make sure the oil is from a reputable company and is suitable for ingestion. Essential oils are very concentrated, and as such, a small amount is recommended. If one drop is too strong, dip a clean toothpick into the bottle and stir it into the recipe. Taste, and decide if you want to add more flavor. Essential oils have a wide scope of properties. I am listing a fraction of them. Please read more to find out their amazing gifts (see bibliography for references).

- **Cinnamon oil** is beneficial for colds, coughs, digestion and flu, and enhances the properties of other oils. No tested virus, bacterium, or fungi survived in the presence of this oil.

- **Fennel oil** is calcium and potassium rich and contains the most powerful anti-oxidant of the vitamin E family. Antioxidants are enzymes, minerals, or vitamins that help protect the body from the formation of free radicals (highly reactive molecules capable of damaging cells and tissue) which can lead to degenerative diseases. Fennel is helpful for cleansing the body and treating spastic colon, sluggish kidneys, worm infestation, constipation, digestion, flatulence, vomiting, and nausea.

- **Ginger oil** is used for sore throats, coughs, fevers, flu, indigestion, chills, cramps, motion sickness, loss of appetite, and in tonics to strengthen the heart and relieve head congestion.

- **Oregano oil** is practically a medicine chest in an herb. Among its many uses, oil of oregano dramatically strengthens the immune system, and is used to treat infections and parasites.

- **Rosemary oil** improves mental alertness, is useful for combating fatigue, colds, and Candida, and decongests the liver. Avoid using this essential oil if you are pregnant or have epilepsy.

- **Sage oil** is great for neutralizing reactions to fats and oils. A powerful antioxidant, sage oil protects fats from degenerating and is used for glandular disorders and bacterial infections. Sage essential oil may also be beneficial for metabolism, the respiratory system, the liver, and digestion. Avoid using sage if you are pregnant or have epilepsy.

- **Wild mint** soothes digestion and supports the lower intestine. It is used to treat hot flashes, migraine headaches, throat infection, toothaches, and food poisoning.

Flower Essences

Essence of Orange Blossom helps control appetite, curbs cravings for sweets, improves digestion, helps stop diarrhea, and soothes irritated respiratory tract.

Essence of Lavender has calming effect on nerves and heart, helps insomnia, tension, nervousness, headaches, digestive aid for nausea, heartburn, and bad breath.

Essence of Rose Petals helps treat poor circulation, spider veins, easy bruising. This fragrant essence aids in digestive, skin and menstrual disorders, and is useful for stubborn coughs, congestion, and respiratory disorders.

These are the real deal, not the frozen, canned product.

Black cherry concentrate, used as blood tonic, is dark and delicious.

Tart cherry concentrate is made from tart Montmorency cherries, and is high in potassium and melatonin. This concentrate is valued for its antioxidant properties. Tart cherries act as a pain reliever for joints, build heart strength, and improve the immune system. The concentrate contains perillyl alcohol, a natural compound that shuts down the growth of cancer cells by depriving them of the proteins they need to grow.

Great Grains

Grains are an excellent source of fibre, unsaturated fatty acids, lecithin, and complex carbohydrates. Grains are also rich in the vitamin B complex. However, this vitamin is destroyed easily by heat. Grains also contain phytin, which when sprouted become more easily metabolized by the body. Sprouting is the best way to enjoy the full nutrient value of grains. For great grains, follow this sprouting method:

1 To remove mould, soak the amount of grain needed for five to 10 minutes in two parts water to one part hydrogen peroxide (3% strength solution will do), then rinse.

2 Soak for 8 to 12 hours in filtered water and rinse.

3 Sprout the grains for one to three days. Rinse the grain in a large strainer or colander, two or three times a day, to keep moist, and keep covered with a towel.

Basic Porridge

Blend the following:

I cup (250 ml) **sprouted grain of your choice**

I½ cups (375 ml) **hot or cold water** (less if a thicker porridge is desired)

Garnish with nut or seed milk, soaked seeds, and fresh or soaked dried fruit.

To make sprouted flour, dry the sprouted grains in a dehydrator. These grains can be ground into flour and used to make a creamy cereal. They don't have to be cooked to be enjoyed. Blend with warm or hot water to make a smooth porridge that resembles cream of wheat.

Grains that are alkaline include: amaranth, millet, quinoa, and teff. These tiny grains will soak and sprout quickly. Rinse the grain in the diluted hydrogen peroxide solution, soak for six to eight hours, and then put them, rinsed, in the refrigerator. They will sprout overnight and can be used the next day for whatever recipe you want.

Grains that are acid include: corn, barley, kamut, oats, rice (there are many different and exotic varieties worth tasting), rye, sorghum, wheat. These are heartier grains. I have not gotten rice to sprout. Barley (unpearled, whole grain), oat groats (the whole oat grain), rye, and wheat will sprout. Sprouting these grains takes a good three to four days.

Gluten-free grains include: amaranth, buckwheat (don't let the name fool you, this is actually the fruit of a plant that belongs to the same family as rhubarb and sorrel, and is not related to wheat), corn, millet, quinoa, rice, sorghum, and teff. Buckwheat

is especially tasty soaked, sprouted for a day and put into a dehydrator to make a crunchy kind of cereal. Combined with sunflower and pumpkin seeds treated the same way, it makes a great breakfast or trail mix.

To store grains, use glass containers to keep out the bugs. One recommendation is to initially put the grains into the freezer to kill any eggs left by bugs.

For more information in detail about grains and their properties consult the **Encyclopedia of Natural Healing,** alive Books, Vancouver, BC (see reference section).

Getting the Most from Grains, Nuts and Seeds

Nature protects seeds, nuts and grains from automatically sprouting by covering them with an enzyme inhibitor. This coating soaks off easily. Soaking these foods makes them more digestible. Soak and rinse the amount you want to use for a recipe the day before — and then blend them. One timesaving trick is to soak and rinse nuts, seeds and grains in advance and then store them in small batches in the freezer. Then, if you have a spontaneous desire to make a recipe that requires soaked almonds; for example, all you need to do is take the amount you need from the freezer. Another alternative is to soak and rinse the ingredients you frequently use, and "dry them back." This requires putting the soaked and rinsed ingredients in a dehydrator, and drying them at 105° F (43°C) until thoroughly dried. Store the ingredients in airtight containers. I prefer glass jars. You can also mill these dried ingredients into flour in the blender, to use as a thickener in soups and other recipes.

When grain is spouted it goes through a biological transmutation and becomes a seed — you can toss them in your garden and they will grow. I have done this with old grains and it has produced a very rich, green garden.

Green Powder

Barley Max, blended green powders, spirulina, chlorella

Green powders have a cleansing effect on the blood and help strengthen the immune system. Manufacturers use unique formulas, but almost all green powders are a source of chlorophyll, beta-carotene, nucleic acids (DNA & RNA), and protein for cell renewal. Find the brand of green powder that meets your needs.

Juices of Essential Oils

Juices are less intense in flavor than essential oils.

Juice of oregano improves digestion, metabolism, circulation, and is an excellent physical and mental tonic.

Juice of rosemary is a powerful antioxidant that improves brain function, including memory, and alertness. Rosemary helps reduce fatigue, anxiety, and depression.

Juice of sage balances the nervous system, improves adrenal function, and helps insomnia, indigestion, lowers stress.

(The above information on juices of essential oils is shared with permission from North American Herb & Spice — see resource page)

Lecithin

This emulsifier breaks down fat into smaller droplets and supplies the body with inositol and choline — coenzymes needed for metabolism. Lecithin improves and facilitates the digestion of fat, aids the function of the liver, prevents kidney and gallstones from forming and keeps the arterial lining free from cholesterol.

Liquid Minerals

Blending a liquid into recipe can be more enjoyable than taking a handful of pills. Minerals do come in liquid form. Essential to regulating the water and acid-alkaline balance in the body, minerals are vital to life. They provide structure to our skeletal system and assist in many functions, including nerve impulses. Chelated minerals, bound to amino acids, are the easiest to assimilate. Find the minerals you need in liquid or powdered form and add them to your recipe. If the taste is too strong, put the minerals in a small portion and use the rest of the recipe as a chaser.

Melon

Eating melon alone is well known to maximize digestion. Honeydew, cantaloupe, watermelon, casaba, crenshaw — for decades I have enjoyed a variety of melon juices. Honeydew is one of my favorites.

Maximise digestion with a melon frappe!

Melon smoothies can be made by combining different melons, or enjoying them one at a time. For variety, blend with ice to make a melon frappe.

What about melon seeds? Blend them! Each melon has a seed with a distinct flavor. Honeydew seeds are somewhat bitter. However, when blended and combined with the sweetener of your choice, and thickened with chia gel, flax meal, or hemp seed, honeydew seeds are transformed into a heavenly cream — a sauce if thick, a dressing if thinned, or a soup by adding more blended melon. Serve in fancy glasses.

Cantaloupe seeds are creamier and I enjoy their flavor alone, although they too can be blended with a sweetener and foods rich in EFAs (essential fatty acids) such chia gel, hemp seeds, or flax meal — the synergy of flavors is exquisite.

The following recipes show great ways to use melon seeds:

Creamed Honeydew Seed

Blend the following:
½ cup (125 ml) **honeydew seeds** (not rinsed)
¼ cup (50 ml) **chia gel** (or other thickener)
¼ cup (50 ml) **honeydew**
I lime, juiced
I – 2 tsp (5 – 10 ml) **maple syrup** (optional)

Cantaloupe Dream Cream

Blend the following:
½ cup (125 ml) **cantaloupe seeds**
2 tsp flax meal (or other thickener)
¼ cup (50 ml) chia gel (or other thickener)
¼ cup (50 ml) cantaloupe
I - 2 tsp (5 – 10 ml) **light agave nectar or
raw honey** (optional)

Miso

This fermented bean paste is made from soybeans. Miso is often mixed with grains such as barley, wheat, rice, millet, or azuki bean. It is fermented with a koji (starter yeast) and then aged. Barley miso can be aged for up to three years. Sodium rich, miso can be used as a salty seasoning. Mellow, or light miso, is sweeter and aged for a shorter time. Rich in digestive enzymes, miso helps predigest foods and balance electrolytes. It is also a vegetarian source of vitamin B12. Miso can be used as an alkaline coffee substitute — simply stir into hot water and enjoy. In Japan, miso was found to aid in healing radiation sickness. Do not boil miso, as this kills the beneficial probiotic enzymes.

MSM (Methyl Sulfonyl Methane)

MSM is a naturally occurring, bioavailable source of dietary sulfur, a basic building block of healthy cells. Next to oxygen, water and salt, MSM is the fourth most needed element in both animal and human nutrition. Involved in nearly every metabolic process in the body, it is essential in the regeneration and nourishment of healthy cells. MSM makes the cells more permeable — facilitating the exchange of oxygen, carbon dioxide and nutrients. When there is available MSM, the body replaces old cells with elastic cells, eventually reducing or replacing stiff wrinkled skin. This helps to keep the appearance youthful, as well as to grow stronger hair and nails. Studies have suggested that MSM relieves joint aches. MSM improves many health problems including allergies, asthma, arthritis, poor circulation, lung dysfunction, stomach and digestive tract problems, and malabsorption. Since MSM tastes bitter by itself, and is best combined with a complete vitamin C, it should be added to pineapple, tomato, or orange juice.

Nuts

In general, nuts have a high protein content: from eight to 18 percent. They contain a variety of vitamins and minerals. As an oil-rich food, and one of the best vegetable sources of vitamin E, they are best stored cool or refrigerated as they can go rancid quickly once shelled. Before soaking, nuts are high in healthy fat. Soaking and germination lowers their fat content and makes them more easily digested.

Nuts can be contaminated by mould or liver flukes — to be on the safe side, soak nuts for 10 minutes in a solution of two part water, one part hydrogen peroxide (3% solution is fine). Rinse well and then soak again to remove the enzyme inhibitor that coats them.

- **Almonds** are one of the few nuts that are alkaline and high in L-lysine (an amino acid). Rich in vitamins A, C, and E, they are also high in selenium, calcium, potassium, magnesium, and phosphorus, as well as protein. Almonds are said to lower cholesterol and promote heart health. Cancer clinics around the world recommend eating almonds daily because of their laetrile content, which acts as an anti-cancer agent.
- **Brazil nuts** are full of significant levels of nutrients, including fibre, protein, niacin, vitamin E, calcium, zinc potassium, and copper. As a source of arginine (an amino acid) this nut helps to play a role in blood clot formation. The linolenic acid present converts to omega-3 fatty acids in the body.
- **Cashews** are rich in copper, magnesium, iron, and phosphorus. This nut is soft, easy to blend, and heavenly as a nut butter. Cashews are not widely available in truly raw form. Most "raw" cashews have been heated or treated before finding their way to our tables. Check the resource page at the back of this book for help finding raw nuts.
- **Hazelnuts**, sometimes mistakenly called filberts, are chock full of phosphorous, potassium, magnesium, selenium, vitamin E, and dietary fibre. Filberts are actually a cultivated variety of European hazelnut and are slightly larger than hazelnuts. Containing plant sterols, these nuts are

believed to play a role in the prevention of a variety of diseases, including heart disease and colon cancer.

- **Macadamia nuts**, originating from Australia, are now also grown in Hawaii. They are rich in antioxidants, calcium, vitamin E and fibre. High in fat, macadamia nut oil has more beneficial omega-3 fatty acid than olive oil. It is reported that a daily dose of these nuts can reduce cholesterol.
- **Pecans**, a member of the hickory family, are rich in the unsaturated fats that help lower cholesterol levels, according to recently published studies. High in zinc, this nut contains over 19 vitamins and minerals. One ounce of pecans provides 10 percent of our daily requirement of fibre.
- **Pine nuts** are mildly laxative and are helpful in treating constipation, as well as dry coughs and dizziness. They lubricate the lungs and intestines, increasing the flow of bodily fluids.
- **Pistachio nuts** help to purify the blood, lubricates the intestines, and are helpful in relieving constipation. Pistachios are considered an important tonic for the whole body.
- **Walnuts** are referred to as "brain food," by some, both for their shape and high oil content. Rich in oils and fats, nuts are best eaten raw, as their oils become less digestible when heated.

Always include nuts in your daily diet. They are "brainfood" providing the beneficial fats and oils.

Nut Butters

When buying nut butters, raw are the most nutritious. Most nut butters have not been presoaked to remove the enzyme inhibitor, so they may be hard to digest for some individuals. One suggestion is to take digestive enzymes when eating nut butters.

Nutritional Yeast

Nutritional yeast is rich in vitamin Bs, phosphorus, and iron, as well selenium, zinc, and chromium — which helps to activate the body's ability to metabolize sugar. Nutritional yeast also contains 40 percent high quality protein. This fine yellow powder has a wonderful nutty flavor and is great as a thickener for gravies and dressings. It is best when combined with calcium-rich foods like sesame or sunflower seeds. I prefer Red Star nutritional yeast, as it is less bitter than other varieties.

Oils

Almond, coconut, flaxseed, grapeseed, hemp seed, olive, sesame and sunflower are healthy, highly functional oils. As with any perishable food, oils stay fresher in the refrigerator. The exception is coconut oil, which may be kept in temperatures of up to 110°F (43°C). Use unrefined, cold pressed, organic oils whenever possible as they are a concentrated food. One tablespoon of olive oil contains approximately 44 olives.

Protein Powders

A wide variety of protein powders are available in stores. Soy is one of the most popular ingredients in protein powders. Goat milk protein is an alternative protein source for those sensitive to soy products. Hemp protein powder is another vegetable-based alternative.

Psyllium Husk

Psyllium Powder is made from the seed husk of East Indian plantain. Psyllium is high in both fibre and mucilage. It can be used as a thickener; a teaspoon will thicken most individual servings (2 cups). Start with small amounts and add more as needed, as it sets quickly. Psylliam is useful as a mild bulk-forming laxative.

Rice Bran Solubles

Rice bran solubles are derived by removing the indigestible fibre from rice bran. There are over 100 known antioxidants in rice bran solubles. This food contains naturally occurring selenium (a natural immune builder), CoQ10 (brain clarity enhancing nutrients), 28 unnamed tocotrienols and various tocopherols (from vitamin E) — all forming a wealth of anti-oxidants to help the body when exposed to viral or bacterial infections. Rice bran solubles contains perfect chains of essential fatty acids and amino acids, as well as major and trace minerals — including calcium, potassium, magnesium, phosphorus, iron, zinc, manganese, copper and iodine. Vitamins A, B (1,2,5 and 6), C, D, E, folic acid biotin, choline, and inositol are also found in this highly nutritious food.

Royal Jelly

This product is more potent than bee pollen. Royal jelly is famous for halting impotence and improving hormone balance. It is also used to rejuvenate, improve the appearance of skin, and slow aging. Royal jelly is a rich source of pantothenic acid (vitamin B), which is essential for proper function of adrenal glands and helps fight stress, fatigue, nervousness, and panic attacks.

Sea Salt

The numerous trace minerals in this salt activate salivary amylase, the digestive enzyme in the mouth. This is important in the primary process of digestion and absorption. Find whole salts; avoid over processed table salts. Sea salt can help correct excess acidity, relieve allergies and skin diseases, and restore digestion. Sea salt provides a steady boost in cellular energy, giving the body heightened resistance to infections and bacterial diseases. Adequate salt in the diet is important to electrolyte balance, as it helps the body to absorb and release moisture.

Sea Vegetables

Powdered dulse, kelp and nori are great seasonings, as well as a good source of virtually fat-free vegetable protein, calcium, magnesium, iodine, and other trace minerals. Dulse is 22 percent protein, kelp is 16 percent, and nori is 28 percent. Powdered seaweeds and sea vegetables are easy to blend into recipes.

Seeds

High in protein, essential fatty acids and fibre, seeds make an excellent addition to any diet.

- **Chia seeds** are a good source of omega-3 and omega-6, boron and calcium. They help to retain moisture in the body, treat constipation and improve endurance. Both flaxseed and chia seeds can be used without soaking. Chia can be used as a thickener. It will soak up quite a bit of liquid if not pre-soaked. When flax and chia are soaked they turn into a gel like substance and need no rinsing.

Chia Gel

I part chia seed
6 parts water (less if a thicker gel is desired)

Put ingredients into a glass jar with a tight fitting lid.

Shake until it sets up into a gel (5-10 minutes).

Store in the refrigerator.

- **Flaxseed products** are rich in omega-3, which is beneficial for the brain, hormonal system, nervous system and liver. Golden flaxseed is preferred. Flaxseed is used to relieve pain and inflammation, cleanse the heart and arteries, strengthen immunity, and improve spleen and pancreas function. Flaxseed is a good source of fibre, acting as an intestinal "broom." Flax products, especially flax meal, should be used immediately. Note the date on oil batches; oil can be frozen to preserve freshness

- **Hemp seed** contains the ideal ratio of EFAs — one part omega-3 to three parts omega-6 and 9. Hemp seed is the highest natural source of GLA (gamma linolenic acid) which has strong anti-inflammatory properties. Containing 25 to 36 percent protein, consuming hemp seed helps to build strong nails, skin, hair, muscles, and connective tissue. Hemp seed products keep best in the refrigerator. Pay attention to expiration dates.

- **Pumpkin seed** strengthens the immune system, as it is rich in zinc and omega-3 fatty acids. A vermifuge (eliminates worms), this simple seed is also used for motion sickness, nausea, and swollen prostate glands.

- **Sesame seed** can be both light beige and black. High in calcium, this seed strengthens the liver and kidneys. Sesame helps to relieve rheumatism, constipation, ringing in the ears, lower backache, weak knees, headache, and numbness. It is said that prematurely graying hair can darken with the consumption of sesame seeds. Sesame is best eaten ground, as they are too small to chew. Once hulled, sesame should be refrigerated, as it turns rancid quickly. The seeds do get bitter if soaked and sprouted for too long. I find that soaking overnight, rinsing, and sprouting for a day is sufficient to avoid the bitter taste. Raw tahini is made from sesame seeds. Light as well as a black raw sesame tahini is commercially available. See resource page.

- **Sunflower seed** is rich in protein and calcium: two tablespoons contain six grams of protein. This seed lubricates the intestines, and has a high polyunsaturated fatty acid content. Once shelled, sunflower seed goes rancid quickly — so use immediately or refrigerate. When soaked, a hull like coating separates from the seed and is best rinsed off. One method is to float the hulls off by soaking in a large bowl, adding water and letting the hulls float to the top, and then pour them off with the excess water. Skimming with a strainer is another method of removing the hulls once they float to the top.

Sweeteners

Natural alternatives to white refined sugar include agave nectar, black strap molasses, date sugar, malt barley, grade B maple syrup, maple sugar, maple cream, rapadura (squeeze dried sugar cane), raw honey, rice syrup, stevia (liquid or powder) and sucanat.

- **Agave nectar** and **tequila** are made from the same plant. Agave nectar tastes similar to honey. There are two flavors, light and dark.
- **Blackstrap molasses** (organic) is the residue left behind when sugar is extracted from sugar cane or sugar beets and refined. It contains vitamin B, and is a rich source of useable iron. Molasses is a proven remedy for arthritis and wrist stiffness.
- **Date sugar** is made from dehydrated dates. A simple fruit-based sugar, rich in minerals, date sugar is less sweet than pitted or soaked dates.
- **Honey** is best used raw — it should say uncooked or untreated on the container. Tupelo honey is the easiest honey to digest. It is said to be the lowest on the glycemic index. Honey contains modest amounts of many vitamins, enzymes, and minerals. Its ability to absorb moisture makes it a good antibacterial agent, as bacteria need moisture to thrive.
- **Malt barley**, made from barley, is a thick, dark sweetener with a mild flavor. However, it is not suitable for gluten-free diets.
- **Maple syrup, maple sugar**, and **maple cream** are all products made from the sap of the maple tree. Grade B is the richest in minerals, and therefore usually recommended for food value. Grade A, also very tasty, has a lighter flavor. If you have never tried maple cream it is well worth a taste.
- **Rapadura** is one of the least processed sugar cane products.
- **Rice syrup**, a gluten free sweetener, is mild and thick.
- **Stevia** is a plant based powdered or liquid sweetener. It is one of the safest sweeteners — even for diabetics. Green and white versions of this sweetener are available. Stevia can have an aftertaste, which some people like. NuNaturals' product has the least aftertaste of any brand I have tried so far.
- **Sucanat** is a dehydrated cane sugar juice that is less processed than white sugar.

Baby Foods . . . .

The rule of thumb for baby foods is one food at a time — mono foods. Keep it simple. Blend one food and make that the meal. Babies don't need salt or sugar to make their food palatable. Blended papaya, bananas, apples, and any sweet fruit with a bit of water are perfectly fine.

Some parents like to lightly steam vegetables like carrots, squash, yams, or broccoli and then blend them into a smooth food. Use ¼ cup (50 ml) of the water used for steaming when blending to prepare a thick sauce or soup consistency. If you want to make it creamier add a teaspoon of flax meal, or chia gel, or a spot (½ tsp, 2 ml) of almond, olive, or sesame oil.

There is no rush to feed babies complicated, difficult to digest foods like grains or beans. Babies don't need grains for at least two to three years.

> **"You see things and say "why?" But I dream things that never were and say "why not?"**
>
> George Bernard Shaw

"Fast Food"– the Healthy Wholesome Way

Cranberry Smoothie

Blend:

¼ **cup** (50 ml) **soaked dried cranberries**
(unsugared is best)

½ **cup** (125 ml) **fresh orange juice**

½ **cup** (125 ml) **chia gel** (or other EFA source)

¼ **cup** (50 ml) **raw cashews**

1 **tsp** (5 ml) **fresh lemon juice**

pinch of grated lemon rind (zest)

Brain Builder Smoothie

Blend:

6 walnuts

¼ **cup** (50 ml) **chia gel**
(or other thickener)

¼ **cup** (50 ml) **frozen blueberries**

½ **cup** (125 ml) **papaya**

1 **frozen banana**

1 **lime, juiced**

2 **tbsp** (25 ml) **aloe juice** (or fresh, raw aloe vera)

Fat Flushing Smoothie

Blend:

½ **cup** (125 ml) **pear slices**

½ **cup** (125 ml) **apples slices**

½ **cup** (125 ml) **soaked raisins**

½ **cup** (125 ml) **raisin soaking water**

½ - 1 **banana**

¼ **tsp** (1 ml) **allspice or pumpkin pie spice**

Raspamatazz Smoothie

Blend:

½ **cup** (125 ml) **frozen raspberries**

½ **cup** (125 ml) **frozen blackberries**

1 **frozen banana**

1 **tsp** (5 ml) **organic lemon rind** (zest)

¼ - ½ **cup** (50 - 125 ml) **pineapple juice**

2 **tsp** (25 ml) **flax meal** (or other thickener)

...nberry Smoothie

Pretty Nutty Smoothie

Blend:

½ **cup** (125 ml) **orange juice**

¼ **cup** (50 ml) **unsalted pistachio nuts** (or other nut)

2 - 3 fresh apricots (pitted, or other fresh pitted fruit)

6 - 8 ice cubes

2 drops essential oil of ginger (optional)

1 packet of Emergen-C (cranberry, raspberry, orange or tangerine flavored- optional)

Sunny Smoothie

Blend:

½ **cup** (125 ml) **soaked sunflower seeds** (rinsed)

½ **cup** (125 ml) **fresh orange juice**

2 dried pineapple rings (soaked)

¼ **cup** (50 ml) **pineapple soaking water**

1 tbsp (25 ml) **pitted dates**

1 - 2 tbsp (25 – 50 ml) **Barley Max** (optional)

Berry Cherry Lemonade

Blend:

⅓ **cup** (75 ml) **fresh lemon juice**

2 - 3 tbsp (25 – 50 ml) **tart cherry concentrate**

⅓ **cup** (75 ml) **frozen raspberries**

1 tbsp (15 ml) **raw honey** (or desired sweetener)

6 - 8 ice cubes

1 cup (250 ml) **water**

2 drops essential oil of mint (optional)

1 packet of Emergen-C, raspberry flavored (optional)

Mango Moments Smoothie

Blend:

½ **cup** (125 ml) **fresh or frozen mango**

1 cup (250 ml) **apple juice** (fresh is best)

2 tbsp (25 ml) **raw macadamia butter**

¼ **cup** (50 ml) **hemp seeds or flax meal**

tty Nutty Smoothie

Berry Cherry Lemonade

Movin' Right Along Smoothie

Blend:

4 soaked prunes

½ **cup** (125 ml) **prune soaking water**

banana

6 walnuts

2 tsp (10 ml) **flax meal** (or other thickener)

½ - I **banana**

2 tbsp (25 ml) **tart cherry concentrate**

Peachy Keen Smoothie

Blend:

½ **cup** (125 ml) **frozen peach**

¼ **cup** (50 ml) **frozen strawberries**

I **frozen banana**

½ **cup** (125 ml) **pineapple coconut juice**

peaches

Apple Sapple Smoothie

Blend:

I **cup** (250 ml) **apple slices**

2 tbsp (25 ml) **raw almond butter**

2 tsp (10 ml) **hemp seeds** (or other thickener)

½ **cup** (125 ml) **hot or warm water**

¼ **tsp** (I ml) **nutmeg**

persimmons

Persimmon Pizzazz Smoothie

Blend:

I **ripe persimmon**

¼ **cup** (50 ml) **pumpkin seeds**

2 soaked figs

½ **cup** (125 ml) **fig soaking water**

I **banana**

¼ **tsp** (I ml) **cardamom** (optional)

2 drops of essential oil of cinnamon (optional)

Try these recipies when you need an extra boost:

Sprouted Smoothie

Blend:

¼ **cup** (50 ml) **clover sprouts** (or other sprouts)

¼ **cup** (50 ml) **sunflower sprouts**

2 **tbsp** (25 ml) **raw almond butter**

½ **cup** (125 ml) **orange juice**

I **banana**

I - 2 **tbsp** (15 – 25 ml) **protein powder of choice**

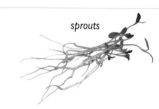
sprouts

Digest-ease Smoothie

Blend:

½ **cup** (125 ml) **papaya**

¼ **cup** (50 ml) **aloe juice**

½ **cup** (125 ml) **chia gel** (or other thickener)

½ **cup** (125 ml) **pineapple juice**

I - 2 **tsp** (5 –10 ml) **green powder of choice**

I **tsp** (5 ml) **mellow white miso** (or sweet miso of choice)

ginger

Nice Green Machine Drink

Blend:

¼ **cup** (50 ml) **wheat grass juice**

¼ **cup** (50 ml) **fresh apple juice**

½ **cup** (125 ml) **carrot juice**

I - 2 **tbsp** (15 – 25 ml) **spirulina** (or other source of chlorophyll)

½ **tsp** (2 ml) **fresh ginger**

2 **drops essential oil of ginger** (optional)

Sprouted Smoothie

Flax Crackers

1 cup (250 ml) **water**

2 cups (500 ml) **mixed seasonal vegetables** (bell peppers, celery, garlic, green beans, onions, spinach, tomatoes, squash)

2 tsp **miso** (10 ml)

1 tsp (5 ml) **sea salt**

2 cups (500 ml) **golden or brown flaxseeds, soaked until they are of a gel-like consistency.**

½ - 1 cup (125 – 250 ml) **chia or hemp seeds** (optional)

Spices to taste (such as Italian, Mexican, poultry seasoning, sea salt, garlic, caraway seeds)

Blend water, vegetables, miso and sea salt.

Stir wet ingredients into soaked flaxseeds, mix well, and pour onto teflex sheets. Sprinkle spices on top. Score into crackers, or drop as round crackers.

Dry at 105° F (43°C) for six to 12 hours, and re-score and turn over. Dry on second side for six to eight hours, or until thoroughly dry.

Store in air tight containers, or thick plastic bags.

Flax "Sourdough" Bread

If you're looking for bread that is yeast-free, gluten-free, and oil-free, this bread created by Victoria and Victor Boutenko fits the bill. It can be fermented for one to three days. This bread can be made chewy or dry and more like a cracker. I think of this recipe as a salad and bread combined in one — a great traveling food. You will need a dehydrator for this recipe..

Wet ingredients:

2 cups (500 ml) **water**

2 stalks celery

I cup (250 ml) **green beans**

2 tomatoes (red or yellow)

I onion (white, red, or yellow)

2 cloves fresh garlic

2 - 4 tbsp (25 – 50 ml) **miso**

Optional: bell peppers, cilantro, dill weed, green onions, parsley, romaine, spinach, or any other vegetable you want to blend

Dry ingredients:

2 cups (500 ml) **flax meal**

I cup (250 ml) **dry chia seeds** (optional)

I cup (250 ml) **hulled hemp seeds** (optional)

Blend wet ingredients.

Mix wet and dry ingredients together in a large bowl, cover with towel and let sit and ferment for one to three days. Form into long thin loaves on teflex sheets, dry at 105° F (43°C) degrees in a dehydrator — turning over after 12 to 18 hours. Dry other side for 6 to 12 hours, or until thoroughly dry.

Pulse these recipes for a chunky salsa. If you want more chunks, take some of the ingredients out and mince — add to the recipe after blending.

Mellow Salsa

2 yellow tomatoes

½ yellow bell pepper

1 tsp (5 ml) turmeric

¼ cup (50 ml) yellow or red onion

½ cup (125 ml) fresh corn kernels

1 - 2 cloves fresh garlic

1 lemon, juiced

Sea salt to taste

red onion

Mango Salsa

1 cup (250 ml) mango

½ cup (125 ml) papaya

½ cup (125 ml) cilantro

¼ cup (50 ml) red onion

2 - 4 tbsp (25 – 50 ml) fresh orange juice

1 drop essential oil of cinnamon
(or fresh cinnamon to taste)

Salsa Verde

4 sliced tomatillos (found in Mexican markets - they look like small green tomatoes, wrapped in a brownish paper-like covering. To use, remove outer coating and rinse inner green fruit)

¼ cup (50 ml) cucumber

¼ cup (50 ml) parsley

1 avocado

2 limes, juiced

1 drop essential oil of oregano
(or fresh oregano to taste)

Mellow Salsa

For pesto, put the greens into the blender first and finely chop, then add the other ingredients to blend together. You can blend the greens first, and then the other ingredients separately and stir them together in a bowl for a different consistency.

Minty Pesto

1 cup (250 ml) **parsley**	**2 cloves fresh garlic**
¼ cup (50 ml) **fresh mint leaves**	**¼ - ½ cup** (50 - 125 ml) **almond or grape seed oil**
2 limes juiced	**sea salt to taste**

garlic

Blushing Tomato Pesto

¼ cup (50 ml) **fresh tomatoes**	**¼ cup** (50 ml) **olive pieces** (pitted)
½ cup (125 ml) **soaked dried tomatoes**	**1 - 2 fresh garlic cloves**
	½ cup (125 ml) **olive oil**
1 cup (250 ml) **fresh sweet basil**	**Sea salt to taste**

fennel

avocado

Dilly Pesto

½ cup (125 ml) **fresh dill**	**½ avocado**
½ cup (125 ml) **parsley**	**½ cup** (125 ml) **grapeseed or sesame oil**
¼ cup (50 ml) **caraway seeds**	**1 drop essential oil of fennel** (or freshly ground fennel seeds)

Minty Pesto

Mellow Yellow Dressing

Blend:

1 cup (250 ml) **pineapple juice**

½ cup (125 ml) **fresh pineapple**

3 - 4 tbsp (50 – 65 ml) **raw macadamia butter**

½ cup (125 ml) **thick chia gel** (or other thickener)

½ tsp (2 ml) **fresh minced ginger root**

1 drop **essential oil of ginger** (optional)

ginger

pineapple

Berry Cherry Dressing

Blend:

½ cup (125 ml) **fresh or frozen raspberries**

2 tbsp (25 ml) **tart cherry concentrate**

¼ cup (50 ml) **apple cider vinegar**

½ cup (125 ml) **olive or grapeseed oil**

1 - 2 tbsp (15 - 25 ml) **agave nectar or raw honey** (optional)

pinch of sea salt

raspberries

Ginger - Miso Dressing

Blend:

¼ cup (50 ml) **raw tahini**

¼ cup (50 ml) **water**

¼ cup (50 ml) **lemon juice**

2 tsp (10 ml) **fresh ginger root**

2 tsp (10 ml) **red or barley miso**

1 tsp (5 ml) **raw honey** (optional)

1 drop **essential oil of ginger** (optional)

Nutty Carrot Dressing

Blend:

1 - 2 tbsp (15 - 25 ml) **raw almond butter**

½ cup (125 ml) **carrot juice**

2 tbsp (25 ml) **fresh or dried dill**

1 **lemon, juiced**

sea salt to taste

Lean Italian Dressing

Blend:

¼ **cup** (50 ml) **water**

¼ **cup** (50 ml) **fresh lemon juice**

1 **tsp** (5 ml) **sea salt**

½ **tsp** (2 ml) **marjoram**

½ **tsp** (2 ml) **oregano**

½ **tsp** (2 ml) **dried sweet basil**

(**Or replace above four spices with 2 tsp** (10 ml) **poultry spice**)

1 **clove fresh garlic**

1 **green onion**

1 **drop essential oil of rosemary** (optional)

To thicken add: ¼ **cup** (50 ml) **thick chia gel or other thickener**

Sweetheart Dressing

Blend:

½ **fresh papaya**

¾ **cup** (175 ml) **fresh orange juice**

¼ **cup** (50 ml) **lime juice**

¼ **cup** (50 ml) **hemp or flax seeds**

pinch of salt

pinch of blended and dried papaya seeds (optional)

y Carrot Dressing

Sublime Summer Soup

Blended Broth:

1 cup (250 ml) **fresh orange or tangerine juice**

½ cup (125 ml) **raw macadamia nuts**

½ cup (125 ml) **chia gel** (or other thickener)

Add: 2 cups (500 ml) **diced: avocado, oranges and strawberries**

strawberries

oranges

Creamy Fruit Soup

Blend:

½ cup (125 ml) **soaked figs**

½ cup (125 ml) **soaked raisins**

1 cup (250 ml) **soaking water**

½ cup (125 ml) **yogurt** (cow, goat, soy)

2 tbsp (25 ml) **soaked pitted dates**

1 tsp (5 ml) **sweet yellow miso** (sweet miso of choice)

Melon Moments Soup

Blended Broth:

2 cups (500 ml) **melon of choice**

Add:
2 cups (500 ml) **Melon balls**

2 - 4 fresh mint leaves

Creamy Corn Gazpacho

Blended Broth:

1 - 1½ cup (250 - 375 ml) **tomato juice or blended fresh tomatoes**

1 **clove fresh garlic**

4 - 6 **soaked dried tomatoes**

¼ cup (50 ml) **flax meal**

juice of 1 lime

pinch of salt

Stir in:

1 cup (250 ml) **diced celery, cucumber, jicama, tomatoes**

1 cup (250 ml) **corn kernels** (cut off raw corn stalk)

¼ cup (50 ml) **minced cilantro**

tomatoes

jicama

Creamy Carrot Soup

Blend:

1 - 1½ cup (250 - 375 ml) **carrot juice**

½ - 1 **avocado**

¼ cup (50 ml) **chia gel** (or other thickener)

¼ cup (50 ml) **fresh basil** (or dill)

1 tbsp (15 ml) **Barley Max** (optional)

a squeeze of lime juice

cucumbers

Minty Raita Soup

Blended Broth:

1 - 1½ cup (250 - 375 ml) **yogurt** (cow, goat, soy)

1 tbsp (15 ml) **fresh lemon juice**

2 - 4 **fresh mint leaves**

1 **drop essential oil of peppermint**

Stir in:
2 cups (500 ml) **thinly cut cucumbers**

¼ cup (50 ml) **minced cilantro**

*Creamy Corn
Gazpacho*

Sweet Potato Soup

Blend:

½ **baked sweet potato**

1 **plantain baked, or banana (unbaked)**

¼ **cup** (50 ml) **chia gel** (or other thickener)

¼ - ½ **cup** (50 - 125 ml) **hot water**

pinch of cinnamon

1 - 2 **drops essential oil of cinnamon**

bananas

sweet potato

Gingerly Carrot Soup

Blend:

1 **cup** (250 ml) **steamed carrots**

1 **cup** (250 ml) **water from steaming carrots**

1 **tbsp** (15 ml) **raw almond butter**

1 **tsp** (5 ml) **mellow yellow miso**

1 **tsp** (5 ml) **fresh ginger root**

1 - 2 **drops essential oil of ginger** (optional)

carrots

Steamed Cauliflower Soup

Blend:

1 **cup** (250 ml) **steamed cauliflower**

2 **stalks celery**

1 **green onion** (scallion)

1 **cup** (250 ml) **water from steaming cauliflower**

1 **clove fresh garlic**

1 - 2 **tsp** (5 - 10 ml) **barley or red miso**

eet Potato Soup

Beets Tahini Sauce

Blend:

½ cup (125 ml) **raw tahini**

¼ cup (50 ml) **grated beets**

¼ - ½ cup (50 - 125 ml) **fresh lemon juice**

¼ - ½ cup (125 ml) **water**

I **stalk celery**

¼ cup (50 ml) **fresh parsley**
(flat leaf parsley works well)

beets

Red Pasta Sauce

Blend:

I cup (250 ml) **fresh diced tomatoes**

½ cup (125 ml) **soaked dried tomatoes**

½ cup (50 ml) **tomato soaking water**

2 **soaked pitted dates**

I **clove garlic**

4 **fresh basil leaves**

I tsp (5 ml) **olive oil**

I - 2 drops **essential oil of Rosemary** (optional)

Spicy Carrot Sauce

Blend:

1½ cup (375 ml) **carrot juice**

2 – 4 tbsp (25 – 50 ml) **raw almond butter**

I tsp (5 ml) **fresh ginger root**

I tsp (5 ml) **mellow white or yellow miso**

I - 2 drops **essential oil of ginger** (optional)

Optional, for a creamier sauce:
2 tbsp (25 ml) **hemp or flax seeds**

2 tbsp (25 ml) **thick chia gel**

56

ets Tahini Sauce

Blushing Cashew Sauce

Blend:

¾ **cup** (175 ml) **raw cashews**

½ **cup** (125 ml) **fresh orange juice**

I **tbsp** (15 ml) **tart cherry concentrate**

¼ **cup** (50 ml) **hemp or flax seeds**

2 **drops essential oil of cinnamon**

Dreamy Prune Whip

Blend:

12 **soaked prunes**

¼ - ½ **cup** (50 - 125 ml) **prune soaking water**

½ **cup** (125 ml) **raw cashews**

¼ **cup** (50 ml) **fresh orange or tangerine juice**

2 **drops ginger oil** (optional)

Royal Delight Sauce

Blend:

I - 1½ **cup** (250 - 375 ml) **apple juice**

2 - 3 **tbsp** (25-50 ml) **tart cherry concentrate**

I **banana**

I **kiwi**

½ **cup** (125 ml) **pomegranate juice** (optional)

pomegranate

Chocolate Pudding

Blend:

2 bananas

1 tbsp (15 ml) raw macadamia butter

2 soaked, pitted dates

¼ cup (50 ml) soaking water

¼ cup (50 ml) chocolate (chips, or small pieces) or cocoa powder

¼ tsp mint extract or 2 drops essential oil of mint

Garnish with:
fresh mint leaves

Down Under Pudding

Blend:

½ cup (125 ml) pitted dates

¼ - ¾ cup (125 - 175 ml) fresh orange juice

1 avocado

1 kiwi

2 tbsp (25 ml) raw carob powder

kiwi

butter

Papaya Pudding

Blend:

1 cup (250 ml) fresh papaya

2 raw eggs

2 tbsp (25 ml) unsalted butter

¼ cup (50 ml) thick chia gel or other thickener

2 drops essential oil of cinnamon (optional)

Berry Sweet Sorbet

Blend:

I frozen banana

1/4 cup (50 ml) frozen raspberries

I tbsp (15 ml) tart cherry concentrate

I tsp (5 ml) lemon zest

Nutty Tropical Sorbet

Blend:

½ cup (125 ml) frozen mango pieces

½ cup (125 ml) frozen pineapple pieces

¼ cup (50 ml) macadamia nuts

mango

Royal Sorbet

Blend:

I frozen banana

¼ cup (50 ml) frozen strawberries

½ cup (125 ml) frozen blueberries

strawberries

Berry Sweet Sorbet

r e s o u r c e s

for organic extra virgin coconut oil:
Alpha Health Products Ltd.
7434 Fraser Park Dr.
Burnaby, BC V5J 5B9 Canada
800-663-2212 or 604-436-0545
www.alphahealth.ca

for Bali's Sun organic extra virgin coconut oil:
Jimar Enterprises Ltd.
QC, 888-969-1874 Canada
coco@balissun.com
www.balissun.com

Earth Fire Products
WI; 608-735-4711
Miso products - kikapoo chutney, plus 7 flavors
of miso

Elysa's Raw & Wild Marketplace
CA; 760-251-7488
call about questions for any resource listed in this
book, kitchen supplies, dehydrators, knives, plus
info on resources, other raw recipe books, con-
sulting services, radio programs on
www.healthylife.net available on CD's- Eating
Naturally, with Elysa; Elysa's Raw & Wild Food TV
Shows (available in video and DVD format)

Gold Mine Natural Food Co.
CA; 800-475-3663
www.goldminenaturalfood.com
Golden Flax, raw nut & seed butters, grains, chia
seeds, dried fruit, real raw carob powder, and
much more, ask for their catalog

Herbal Answers
NY; 888-256-3367
e-mail: aloedoc@aol.com
Herbal Aloe Force Juice and Skin Gel - the only
organic ,whole, raw Aloe product - juice and gel

JoAnn & David's Health Products
CA; 800-700-5402
www.msmsupplements.com
many health enhancing products, ask for catalog
- including rice bran solubles, colostrum, protein & green powders, digestive enzymes, bee
pollen,agave nectar

Leland Cherry
WI; 800-939-3199
www.lelandcherry.com
tart Montmorency cherry concentrate

Martins Maple Farm
Vermont 802-875-1271
www.martinsmaplefarm.com
maple syrup products, maple cream

Nature's First Law
CA; 888- 729-3663 or 619-596-7979
www.rawfood.com
supplier of exotic raw foods such as: Raw cashews,
carob, coconut , macadamia butter; plus books,
health products, and more

North American Herbs & Spice
IL; 800-243-5242 or 847-473-4700
www.oreganol.com
edible essential oils, flower essences, food wash,
juices of (essential oils), royal kick, books and more

Nutiva
CA; 800-993-4367
www.nutiva.com
hemp seeds, hemp protein powder, and hemp oil

Rapunzel Pure Organics, Inc.
NY; 800-207-2814
www.rapunzel.com
the best tasting cocoa powder, block bitter sweet
and semi- chocolate - sweetened by rapadura
(squeeze dried cane sugar, also their product), no
hydrogenated oils

The Grain & Salt Society
NC; 800-867-7258
www.celtic-seasalt.com
many varieties of sea salt, and other health products

Tribest
CA; 888-254-7336 or 562-623-7150
www.personalblender.com
e-mail: service @tribest.com
Barley Max, health books, kitchen / food processing
machines, and other health products

*The personal blender
complete with large
250/500ml cup
and carrying case.*

references/ bibliography

Baker, Elizabeth. *Unbelievably Easy Sprouting Book*. Poulsbo, WA: Baker House, 2000.

Conrad, Chris. *Hemp for Health*. Rochester, Vermont: Healing Arts Press, 1997

DeLangre, Jacques, Ph.D. *Seasalt's Hidden Powers*. Magalia, CA: Happiness press, 1994

Fife, Bruce, N.D. *The Healing Miracles of Coconut Oil*. Colorado Springs, CO: Piccadilly Books, Ltd. 2001.

Gursche, Siegfried. *Encyclopedia of Natural Healing*. Burnaby, British Columbia: Alive Books Publishing, 1997.

Higley, Alan & Connie. *Reference Guide for Essential Oils*. Spanish Fork, UT: Abundant Health, 1998.

Ingram, Cass, D.O. *The Cure is in the Cupboard*. Buffalo Grove, IL: Knowledge House, 2001

Pitchford, Paul. *Healing with Whole Foods*. Berkeley, CA: North Atlantic Books, 1993.

Sheer, James F. *The Magic of Chia*. Berkeley, CA: Frog, Ltd., 2001.

Shurtleff, William & Aoyagi, Akiko. *The Book of Miso*. Berkeley, CA: Ten Speed Press, 2001.

Rhio. *Hooked on Raw*. New York: Beso Entertainment, 2000.

Wolfe, David. *Eating For Beauty*. Maul Brothers Publishing, San Diego, CA: March, 2002; www.davidwolfe.com

**alive
BOOKS**

Vancouver
Canada

First published in 2003 by
alive Books

7432 Fraser Park Drive
Burnaby BC V5J 5B9
(604) 435–1919
1-800-663-6580
www.alive.com

© 2003 alive books
First Printing - September 2003
Second Printing - September 2004

© 2003 by Elysa Markowitz

Book Design:
    Paul Chau
Artwork:
    Guy Andrews
Food styling & recipe development
    Elysa Markowitz, Christel
    Gursche and Sieglinde Janzen
Photographs:
    Edmond Fong
Photo Editing:
    Ramona Franzen
Editing:
    Judith Comfort
Proofreading/Production:
    Ramona Franzen

Canadian Cataloguing in Publication Data

Elysa Markowitz
    Smoothies!
    and Other Scrumtious Delights.

(alive natural health guides, 36
ISSN 1490-6503)
ISBN 1-55312-041-8

Printed in Canada